Funny Bone Jokes

WEIRD Science JOKES to Tickle Your FUNNY BONE

Felicia Lowenstein Niven

Enslow Elementary
an imprint of

Enslow Publishers, Inc.
40 Industrial Road
Box 398
Berkeley Heights, NJ 07922
USA
http://www.enslow.com

Enslow Elementary, an imprint of Enslow Publishers, Inc.

Enslow Elementary® is a registered trademark of Enslow Publishers, Inc.

Library of Congress Cataloging-in-Publication Data

Niven, Felicia Lowenstein.
  Weird science jokes to tickle your funny bone / Felicia Lowenstein Niven.
       p. cm. — (Funny bone jokes)
  Includes bibliographical references and index.
  Summary: "Includes jokes, limericks, knock-knock jokes, tongue twisters, and fun facts about animals, plants, weather, outer space, recycling, and more, and describes how to create your own funny board game"—Provided by publisher.
  ISBN 978-0-7660-3543-0
  1. Science—Juvenile humor. I. Title.
  PN6231.S4N58 2010
  818'.602—dc22
                          2010004191

Printed in the United States of America

122010 Lake Book Manufacturing, Inc., Melrose Park, IL

10 9 8 7 6 5 4 3 2 1

To Our Readers: We have done our best to make sure all Internet Addresses in this book were active and appropriate when we went to press. However, the author and the publisher have no control over and assume no liability for the material available on those Internet sites or on other Web sites they may link to. Any comments or suggestions can be sent by e-mail to comments@enslow.com or to the address on the back cover.

Every effort has been made to locate all copyright holders of material used in this book. If any errors or omissions have occurred, corrections will be made in future editions of this book.

♻ Enslow Publishers, Inc., is committed to printing our books on recycled paper. The paper in every book contains 10% to 30% post-consumer waste (PCW). The cover board on the outside of each book contains 100% PCW. Our goal is to do our part to help young people and the environment too!

Contents

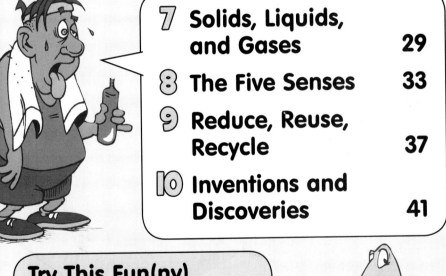

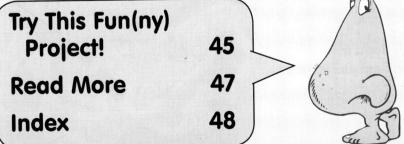

Animals

What is gray, has four legs and a trunk?

A mouse going on a long vacation!

Where does a horse eat his morning cereal?

At the breakfast stable!

Each time you see this squiggly box, it is a tongue twister! Try saying it five times fast!

Fran feeds fish fresh fish food.

What did the hungry dalmatian say when he had a meal?

That hit the spots!

Six shy snails sighed sadly.

OAT TREATOS

FUN FACTS

When most people see a skunk, they run. They don't want to risk getting hit by that bad-smelling spray. But just how far can a skunk shoot its stinky spray? Two yards! That may not seem very far, but you can smell it up to two and a half miles away. And the smell can last for days! Luckily skunks only spray when they're scared or under attack.

IT'S TRUE.

If you cross across a crowded cow crossing, cross the cross cow carefully.

There once were two backcountry geezers
Who got porcupine quills up their sneezers.
They sat beak to beak
For more than a week
Working over each other with tweezers.

Knock, Knock!

Who's there?

Owls

Owls who?

Of course they do, everybody knows that!

FUN FACTS

Have you ever seen a bird fly backwards? If you have, you've seen a hummingbird. They are the only birds that can do that. In fact, it's not just birds. Not every animal can move backwards. An emu and kangaroo are two examples of animals that can't.

IT'S TRUE.

Knock, Knock!

Who's there?

Interrupting Cow

Interrupting Cow wh...

Moo!!!!

What always sleeps with its shoes on?

A horse.

What does a cat have that no other animal has?

Kittens!

What is as big as an elephant, but weighs nothing at all?

The shadow of an elephant!

DID YOU KNOW?

A joke is something that makes people laugh. A riddle gives you clues. You guess the answer. Riddles can really make you think!

IT'S TRUE.

What do you get if you cross a cocker spaniel, a poodle, and a rooster?

Cockerpoodledoo!

Speedy Sam, while exploring a cave,
Had what I call a very close shave.
He stepped on a bear,
That had dozed off in there.
I'm glad he was faster than brave.

② Plants

Knock, Knock!

Who's there?

Lettuce

Lettuce who?

Lettuce in, and you'll find out!

How do trees get onto the Internet?

They log on.

DID YOU KNOW? IT'S TRUE.

A limerick is a funny poem that rhymes. Lines 1, 2, and 5 rhyme one way. Lines 3 and 4 rhyme another.
A tongue twister is a group of words with similar sounds. But try to say them fast. It's very hard to do.

I trimmed up my hedge, as you do
Into animal shapes, like a zoo.
They all looked so real
A neighbor, with zeal
Tried to ride on the green kangaroo!

I planted some tulips last fall.
The wife doesn't like them at all.
They force her to sneeze
And attract bumblebees.
It's driving her right up the wall!

What kind of flower grows on your face?

Tulips!

Twelve pears hanging high, 12 men passing by. Each took a pear and left 11 hanging there. How can 11 pears be left?

"Each" is a man's name!

FUN FACTS

IT'S TRUE.

Take a deep breath. You were able to do that because of a tree. Just one acre of a forest puts out four tons of oxygen. That is enough for eighteen people to breathe for a whole year. But that's not all. Trees provide shade. A young healthy tree can keep us pretty cool. It would take ten room-size air conditioners working twenty hours to do the same. That means you can breathe easy and stay cool.

FUN FACTS

Is it cold outside? Ask your rhododendron. When it drops below 35 degrees, this plant reacts. Its leaves cup and curl. At 25 degrees, the leaves droop. When temperatures are in the teens, the leaves become brownish green. Imagine if we changed color when it was cold!

IT'S TRUE.

If a farmer met a farmer in a farmer's field, how many *f*'s are in that?

None. There are no *f*'s in the word "that."

What kind of tree can fit in your hand?

A palm tree.

What happened to the plant in math class?

It grew square roots.

Little leaves lay lazily in the lane.

Six thick thistle sticks. Six thick thistles stick.

Knock, Knock!

Who's there?

Broccoli

Broccoli who?

Broccoli doesn't have a last name, silly.

③ Insects

Why did the bee fly south for the winter?

To visit an ant in Florida.

How do fireflies start a race?

Ready, set, glow!

What does a caterpillar do on New Year's Day?

Turns over a new leaf!

I don't like butter, and I'm not a fly.
Whoever named me made a bad try.
When I'm not flying up too high,
You might chase me when I flutter
by. What am I?

A butterfly.

Why do bees hum?

Because they've
forgotten the words.

FUN FACTS

How far would you go to get food? A bee may fly up to 60 miles in one day. That's because it takes a lot of trips to collect enough nectar. To make a pound of honey, honeybees make about 10 million trips. They look for pretty flowers. Then they suck out the nectar and pollen. It's a big job. The next time you have honey, thank a bee!

IT'S TRUE.

FUN FACTS

IT'S TRUE.

Some ants can carry more than fifty times their own weight. That is like you carrying a car! And we're not talking about the toy kind! Sometimes ants work together to carry even more. There are over 10,000 different kinds of ants. How much they carry depends on what kind of ants they are.

Knock, Knock!

Who's there?

Weak ant

Weak ant who?

We can't stop laughing at this joke!

A caterpillar moved like a sloth
Till the day he turned into a moth.
Then he zoomed like a jet
To the cupboard to get
His teeth into everyone's cloth!

16

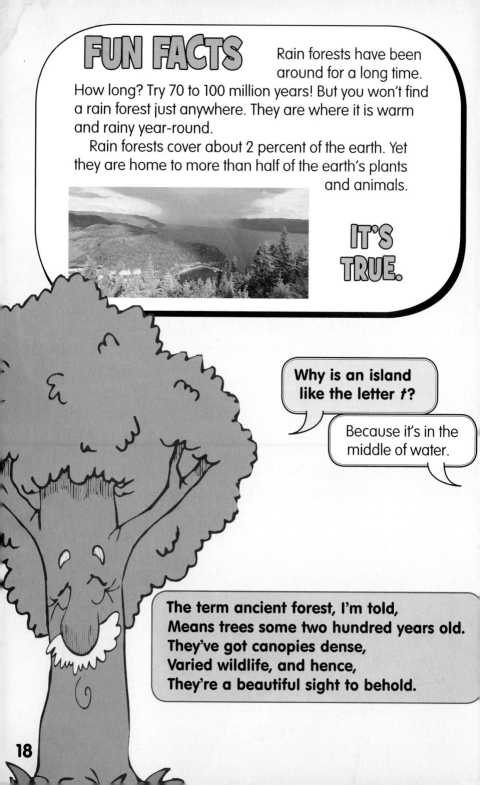

FUN FACTS

Rain forests have been around for a long time. How long? Try 70 to 100 million years! But you won't find a rain forest just anywhere. They are where it is warm and rainy year-round.

Rain forests cover about 2 percent of the earth. Yet they are home to more than half of the earth's plants and animals.

IT'S TRUE.

Why is an island like the letter *t*?

Because it's in the middle of water.

The term ancient forest, I'm told,
Means trees some two hundred years old.
They've got canopies dense,
Varied wildlife, and hence,
They're a beautiful sight to behold.

Cows graze in droves on grass that grows on grooves in groves.

Knock, Knock!

Who's there?

Yukon

Yukon who?

Yukon say that again!

Here's a riddle for students you teach:
"What is soft to the touch, like a peach,
Colored beige, covers land,
Mostly made out of sand?"
All the kids will respond, "It's a beach!"

FUN FACTS

The desert is the driest place on Earth. Deserts get less than ten inches of rain each year. Some deserts may get no rain for many years. That's why some deserts have nicknames. Have you heard of Death Valley in California? It's because most people, animals, and plants can't survive there. There isn't enough water.

IT'S TRUE.

The Weather

What is a tornado's favorite game?

Twister!

Do snowmen use paste to fix things?

No. They use igloo.

DID YOU KNOW?

Meteorology is the study of weather.

IT'S TRUE.

What do clouds wear in their hair?

Rainbows!

You can do a lot of splashing in an inch of rain. But that same amount of water makes a lot more snow. One inch of rain equals 15 inches of powdery snow! So you don't have to have a flood to have a snow day! Just make sure the temperature is less than 32 degrees Fahrenheit. Then, sled on!

IT'S TRUE.

We surely shall see the sun shine soon.

Falling snow is fluffy and light.
It is truly a wonderful sight.
But once turned to slush,
A horrible mush,
I wish it would melt out of sight.

FUN FACTS

IT'S TRUE.

Lightning can strike twice! In fact, it can hit the same place many times. Very tall objects attract lightning. The Empire State Building in New York City measures 1,250 feet. During one thunderstorm it was struck 8 times! That happened in just 24 minutes.

As the weather grew hotter and hotter,
My clothes absorbed sweat like a blotter.
As the temperature rose
From my head to my toes,
I wanted to lie in deep water.

What can clap without any hands?

Thunder.

How much dew would a dew drop drop, if a dew drop did drop dew?

You wouldn't want to live in an oven. It feels hotter on Venus. It is the hottest planet in the universe. Scientists say it is about 864 degrees Fahrenheit. That's because heat comes in but it doesn't leave. The atmosphere traps it there. But Venus isn't as hot as the sun. The center of the sun is about 27 million degrees Fahrenheit.
Now that's hot stuff! **IT'S TRUE.**

> Venus views are very volcanic.

There once was a Martian named Zed
With antennae all over his head.
He sent out a lot
Of di-di-dash-dot,
But nobody knows what he said.

> There's no need to light a nightlight
> on a light night like tonight.

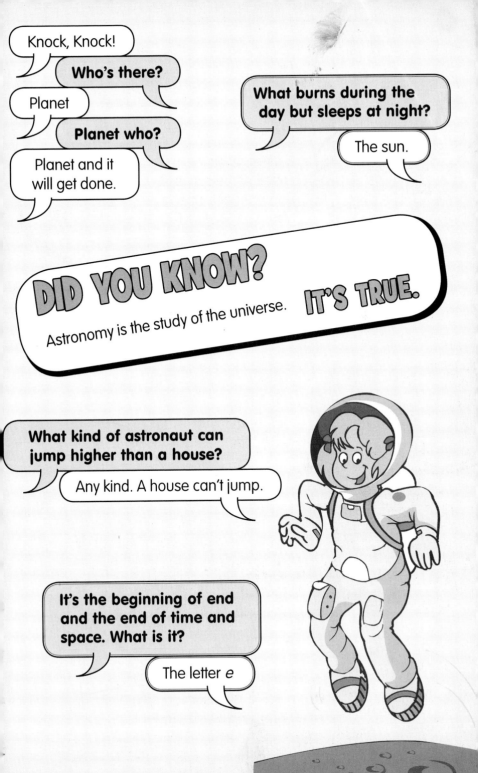

Knock, Knock!

Who's there?

Ida

Ida who?

Ida tough time getting back to Earth!

EARTH

There once was a star so immense
It became incredibly dense,
Then collapsed at great rate
To a terrible fate,
And has been a black hole ever since.

FUN FACTS

Name the largest planet. If you said Jupiter, you're right! It is so large that you could fit 1,400 Earths inside! It is also fast. It takes Jupiter just under ten hours to rotate on its orbit. That's a very short day and not a lot of time to sleep! But don't pack your bags yet. There is no land on Jupiter, just gas. It would also take you a long time to get there. If you could drive, it could be almost 1,000 years.

IT'S TRUE.

While we were walking, we were watching window washers wash Washington's windows with warm water.

There was a young man from Rangoon,
Whose farts could be heard on the moon!
When you least would expect them,
They'd roar from his rectum
With a sound like a double bassoon!

Knock, Knock!

Who's there?

Few

Few who?

Few, what is that smell!

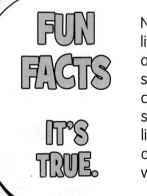

FUN FACTS

IT'S TRUE.

Normal bodies make about a half-liter of gas each day. That is about a quarter of one of those big plastic soda bottles. Where does the gas come from? Some comes from air we swallow. Some comes from bacteria living inside of us. How the gas smells depends on what we eat. Too bad, we can't just eat cotton candy!

When a solid is heated, it changes to a liquid. If it is heated more, it becomes a gas. But sometimes solids go directly to a gas. That happens with dry ice. When you heat dry ice, it changes. It becomes a smoky-looking gas. It is perfect for Halloween or other spooky fun.

IT'S TRUE.

Big Ben blew big blue bubbles.

It's soft, or it's hard, or it's small,
Or it's large; when it's dropped, it'll fall.
It's usually round,
But an oblong one found
In an end zone abounds—it's a ball.

The Five Senses 8

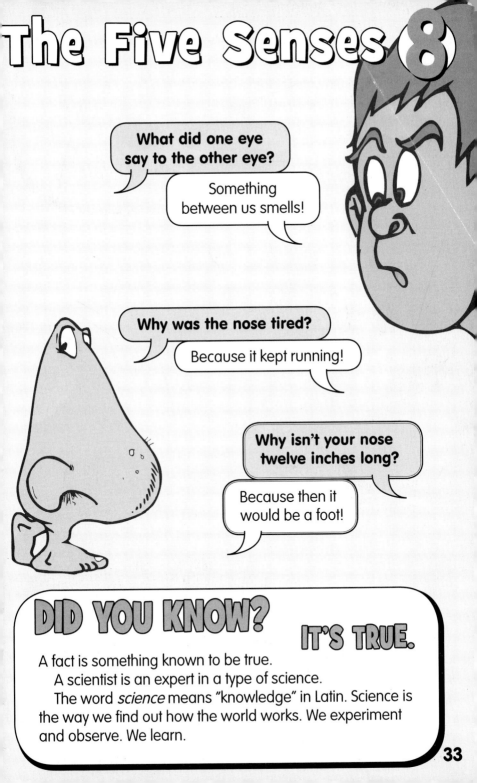

What did one eye say to the other eye?

Something between us smells!

Why was the nose tired?

Because it kept running!

Why isn't your nose twelve inches long?

Because then it would be a foot!

DID YOU KNOW? IT'S TRUE.

A fact is something known to be true.

A scientist is an expert in a type of science.

The word *science* means "knowledge" in Latin. Science is the way we find out how the world works. We experiment and observe. We learn.

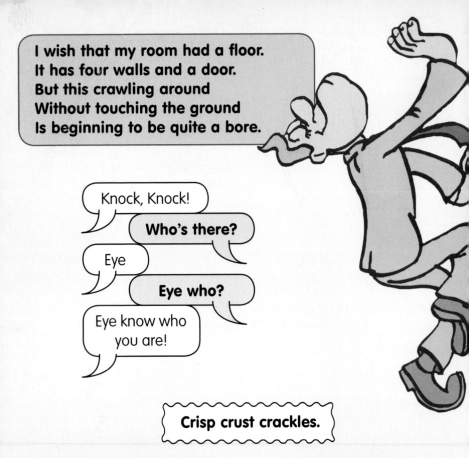

I wish that my room had a floor.
It has four walls and a door.
But this crawling around
Without touching the ground
Is beginning to be quite a bore.

Knock, Knock!

Who's there?

Eye

Eye who?

Eye know who you are!

Crisp crust crackles.

FUN FACTS

IT'S TRUE.

When something tastes good, thank your taste buds. These are tiny cells in your mouth. You have almost 10,000 of them. There are four different kinds of tastes. The salty and sweet buds are near the front of your tongue. Sour is along the side. Bitter is in the back. As you grow older, your taste buds disappear. That's why you might like different food when you're grown up. Tell that to your parents when they suggest you eat spinach!

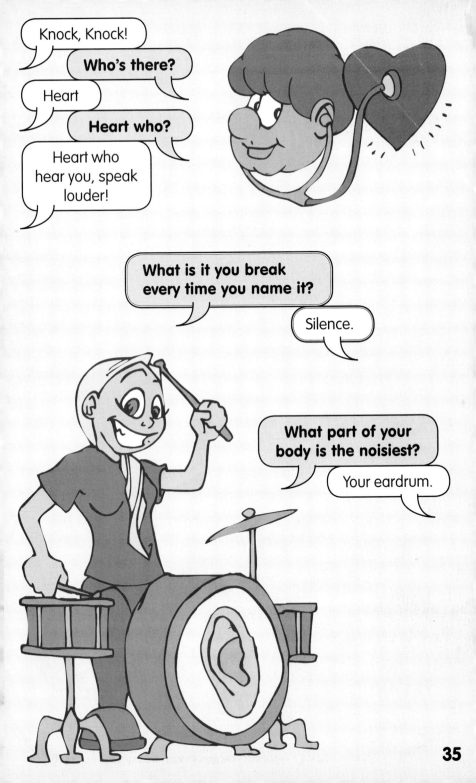

How well do you smell? You can tell the difference between 4,000 scents. You might smell as many as 10,000, but this doesn't last forever. As you get older, you can't smell as well. That's great for kids. But for adults, that stinks! Or maybe it doesn't?

IT'S TRUE.

A noisy noise annoys an oyster.

The little nerve endings in skin
Make one flinch at the prick of a pin,
Or react to an itch,
Or anything which
Causes pressure without or within.

Reduce, Reuse, Recycle

Why did the foolish gardener plant a lightbulb?

He wanted to grow a power plant.

What's black and white and red (read) all over—again and again?

Recycled newspaper!

DID YOU KNOW?

Chemistry is the study of how things are and how they can change.

Physics is the study of how things interact with one another.

IT'S TRUE.

FUN FACTS

Do you recycle? More than one hundred years ago, New Yorkers did. That is when the first recycling program started. New York built a recycling plant in 1898. Americans create the most trash in the world! We could recycle 75 percent of it. It's time to bash the trash!

IT'S TRUE.

Why did the chicken carrying several bags full of separated paper, plastic, glass, and metal cross the road?

To get to a Halloween party dressed as a recycler.

Knock, Knock!

Who's there?

Gladys

Gladys who?

Gladys recycling day, aren't you?

Paper and plastic piles perilously in Peter's place.

Environment's not just a phase.
It's the choice between blue sky and haze.
We can keep the air clear
If we show that we care
By taking the bus every day.

What is a renewable resource used every day at your school?

Brainpower!

How is energy conservation like a baseball team?

They can both use a switch-hitter.

FUN FACTS IT'S TRUE.

Go ahead. Count to a minute. That is how long it takes to make 350,000 cans. No kidding! And if you recycle just one, you save energy. That is enough to run a TV for three hours. Imagine how much you could watch if you recycled all of them!

In 1905, eleven-year-old Frank Epperson mixed soda and water. He accidentally left it outside. Since it was winter, it froze. Frank found it the next day. He licked it. It was delicious! The next summer, he sold his Epsicles. Later he changed the name. He called it Popsicle for the soda pop.

IT'S TRUE.

Ford did not invent the car.
The Germans were quicker by far.
But he found a way
To make hundreds a day,
And that's how things got as they are.

Crazy cars collided continuously.

DID YOU KNOW?

An invention is the creation of something new. **IT'S TRUE.**

FUN FACTS

Do you like to play catch? It's fun with a ball. It's even more fun with empty pie plates. At least, that's what some college kids thought. That gave Walter Frederick Morrison an idea. He invented a plastic plate that could fly pretty far. This was the idea behind a popular toy. It was named after the Frisbie Pie Company. Can you guess? It's the Frisbee by the Wham-O company.

IT'S TRUE.

Tom Edison thought he was bright.
He invented the electric light.
Then, to his chagrin,
When turning in,
His wife said, "I'll be reading tonight."

What was Isaac Newton's brother's name?

Fig.

Knock, Knock!

Who's there?

Disc

Disc who?

Disc is a recorded message!

Try This Fun(ny) Project!

Now that you know a lot of new jokes, you can use them for more than laughs. Here is how to make your own funny board game.

HERE'S WHAT YOU WILL NEED:

- an old game board or a large piece of cardboard
- markers and a pen
- construction paper
- game pieces ("found" items around the house)
- dice

DIRECTIONS:

1. Take an old game board or a large piece of cardboard. You may have to cover the old game board with construction paper.

2. Using the markers, create a space for start and one for finish.

3. Make spaces between start and finish. Label a few spaces "Joke." Label a few spaces "Punch Line." Label a few spaces "Go Back 3." Label a few spaces "Go Ahead 2." Think of your own labels and add them. You can make a "Wild Card" space.

4. Cut the construction paper into the size of playing cards.

5. On each card write a joke on one side. Write the punch line, or answer, on the other.

6. Put the cards in the middle.

7. Find some playing pieces. These could be anything around the house. A paper clip would work. So would a bolt. You might play with a pencil eraser.

8. Choose your piece. Put it at "Start." Now you are ready to play.

9. Roll the dice. Move to a space.

10. When it says "Joke," your opponent reads a joke card. You have to tell him the right answer. If you get it right, you roll again.

11. When it says "Punch Line," your opponent reads just the answer. You have to tell him the joke. If you get it right, you roll again.

12. If you made a Wild Card, you get to tell your own joke. If your partner doesn't know the answer, you roll again.

13. The first person to reach "Finish" is the winner. You should have some good laughs along the way!

Read More

Books

Chmielewski, Gary. *The Science Zone: Jokes, Riddles, Tongue Twisters, and "Daffynitions."* Chicago, Ill.: Norwood House Press, 2008.

Phillips, Bob. *Good Clean Knock-Knock Jokes for Kids*. Eugene, Ore.: Harvest House Publishers, 2007.

Super Clean Jokes for Kids. Uhrichsville, Ohio: Barbour Publishing, 2009.

Weitzman, Ilana, Eva Blank, Rosanne Green, and Alison Benjamin. *Jokelopedia: The Biggest, Best, Silliest, Dumbest Joke Book Ever*. New York: Workman Publishing Company, 2006.

Internet Addresses

Jokes for Kids
<http://www.activityvillage.co.uk/kids_jokes.htm>

NIEHS Kids' Pages: Jokes, and Trivia
<http://kids.niehs.nih.gov/jokes.htm>

Index